Contents

FLAT GREEN BOWLS

The green

Acknowledgements

The publishers would like to thank Drakes Pride for their photographic contribution to this book.

Cover photography and photographs on pages 13 and 29 courtesy of *World Bowls* magazine.
All other photographs courtesy of Allsport UK Ltd.
Illustrations by Tim Bairstow.

Note   Throughout the book players, umpires and scorers are referred to individually as 'he'. This should, of course, be taken to mean 'he or she' where appropriate.

The green should not be longer than 40 m nor shorter than 31 m in the direction of play.

The green is divided into rinks each not more than 5.8 m nor less than 4.3 m wide, numbered consecutively. The four corners of the rinks shall be marked by pegs of wood, painted white and fixed to the face of the bank and flush therewith. These corner pegs shall be connected with green thread drawn tightly along the surface of the green with sufficient loose thread to reach the corresponding pegs on the face of the bank. The pegs and thread define the boundary of the rink. (Boundary threads may be dispensed with.)

The green must be level and surrounded by a ditch and bank. The bank shall not be less than 230 mm above the level of the green, preferably upright or alternatively at an angle of not more than 35 degrees from the perpendicular. The surface of the face of the bank shall be non-injurious to bowls.

Speed of the green

It may sound odd but on what is known as a 'fast' green a bowl takes longer to reach its objective than on a 'slow' green. A bowl needs to be delivered on a line which provides a wide arc of travel; therefore, it has further to go and consequently takes longer to arrive.

A green is said to be 'fast' if:

- its surface is quite firm and hard
- its grass is closely mown
- it has been subjected to long periods of hot sunshine
- it has been well trodden.

(The speed of the green at indoor clubs will vary according to the type of carpet that is in use, as well as to the form of underlay adopted.)

A green is said to be 'slow' if:

- its grass is comparatively long
- its surface is spongy
- there has been recent heavy rainfall.

Such surfaces will demand that a bowler use a much tighter arc to reach his objective. This tighter line means that the bowl does not travel as far, and so it arrives at its destination quicker than it would on a 'fast' green. For instance, a bowl might take 10 or 11 seconds to cover a distance of 27 m on a 'slow' green, whereas on a 'fast' green it might take 14 or 15 seconds to cover the same distance (*see* fig. 1).

Weather conditions will affect all outdoor surfaces, even during the time it takes to complete a game. Every bowler will have to judge such changes in the speed of the green so that he can find the correct line as well as the correct pace.

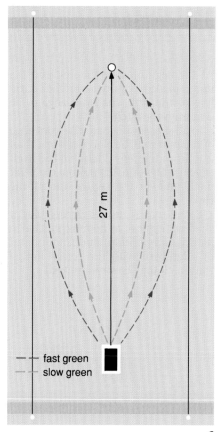

27 m

fast green
slow green

▶ *Fig. 1 The speed of a green will dictate the tightness of the arc a bowler must use to reach the objective*

The mat

The jack and the bowls

At the beginning of the first end the mat is placed lengthwise on the centre line of the rink, the front edge to be 2 m from the ditch.

In all subsequent ends the front edge of the mat shall be placed not less than 2 m from the rear ditch and the front edge not less than 23 m from the front ditch and on the centre line of the rink.

If the mat is moved during play it shall be replaced as near as possible in its original position, and if found out of alignment with the centre line of the rink it may be straightened.

The jack shall be round and white with a diameter of not less than 63 mm nor more than 64 mm, and not less than 225 g nor more than 285 g in weight.

The jack has no bias (*see* page 6). The legal casting of the jack to any position on the rink is a recognised skill. It may be employed such that the distance the jack travels along the rink is that best suited to that particular player. It can also be used to wrest an advantage from an opponent by varying the distance from the mat to the jack. Any player aspiring to become a proficient singles player, or indeed a good lead (*see* page 18), would do well to develop the ability of casting a jack consistently and accurately.

The bowls are of wood, rubber or composition. Each set of bowls is required to carry an individual distinguishing mark.

Some bowls are made of a very hard wood called lignum vitae; such bowls must have a diameter not greater than 134 mm and not less than 116 mm, and must not weigh more than 1.59 kg.

It is an advantage to use as heavy a bowl as possible without overloading the grip. The choice of bowl will therefore be influenced by the size of the player's hand and the particular grip adopted when playing (*see* page 7). Composition bowls are heavier, size for size, than bowls of lignum vitae. Composition bowls are unaffected by temperature changes; lignum vitae bowls, having lost their polish, lose weight on exposure to the sun. Lignum vitae bowls are generally more responsive to bias than composition bowls, and are less affected by heavy greens.

Bowls are made, and should be bought, in sets of four – four bowls is the maximum number any one player in any one game requires.

Choosing your bowls

When buying your bowls remember that:

- the bowl must not be too large for your hand
- a composition bowl is heavier than a lignum bowl
- you will need a set of four
- the set should be a 'matched' set – check by looking for the set number which will be stamped on each bowl
- first quality new bowls are expensive, but a good second-hand set can be obtained at a reasonable price
- a full set will have been cut from the same log – the bowls will be identical in weight and balance, and any variation in weight due to natural shrinkage of the lignum will be uniform
- well-known manufacturers are to be preferred
- the advice of an experienced coach and/or player is invaluable.

Bias

Every bowl has a bias – it is so constructed that when rolled along a level ground it traces a curving path. The amount of the curve increases as the speed of the bowl decreases. With the average speed of delivery of a bowl the effect of the bias is negligible until the bowl has travelled about three-fifths of its distance. From that moment until it comes to rest it curves more and more in response to the bias. To bring a bowl to rest touching the jack, the player must aim to the left or right of it, delivering the bowl with its biased side on the right or the left. The bias side of the bowl will always be on the inside of the curve.

The amount of bias is strictly regulated. It must not be *less* than that approved by the International Bowling Board (IBB), now named World Bowls Board (WBB). Each bowl must have the stamp of the WBB/IBB and/or the British Isles Bowls Council (BIBC) to certify that its bias is not less than the allowable minimum.

Only an official bowl tester may alter the bias of a bowl – a player who changes the bias on a bowl bearing the stamp of the WBB/IBB or the BIBC is liable to suspension from the game.

Point of aim

The effect of the bias on the bowl is negligible until the bowl has covered about three-fifths of its path. From then onwards the bowl follows a curving path, the amount of the curve increasing all the time until the bowl comes to rest. When the bowl has travelled three-fifths of its path it will be at its widest point from the straight line connecting the mat and the jack. This point is known as the 'point of aim' (also known as the 'shoulder' or 'arc').

The area enclosed between the curved path of the bowl and the line from the mat to the jack is known as 'land' (also called 'line', 'width', 'green' or 'grass').

Fixing the point of aim will vary with each bowl sent down the green. It depends upon:

- the length of the jack, i.e. distance from mat to jack
- the bias on the bowl
- wind
- the heaviness of the green – on a wet, heavy green less land will be used than on a dry green
- the trueness of the green – one side of the green might 'draw' (*see* page 22) better than the other side.

Never fail to test the green before beginning play – send down two or three bowls from each end to establish the drawing qualities in both directions and on both sides.

In competitive games a trial end in each direction is permitted before the game commences.

Grip

In the main, there are two basic methods of holding the bowl: the 'claw' and 'cradle' grips. However, there is a large number of variations between the two, depending on the personal preference of the bowler.

Claw grip

The thumb is placed on top of the bowl, or near to the top, so that the bowl is held predominantly by the thumb and fingers, with much of the palm of the hand not in contact with the bowl. The fingers are spread evenly on the underside, reasonably close together. The little finger is occasionally brought up the bowl on the opposite side to the thumb. It is important not to squeeze or overgrip the bowl since this can bring about unnecessary strain to the base of the thumb and to the wrist.

(a)

(b)

▲ *Fig. 2 Claw grip: (a) front view; (b) side view*

Cradle grip

The bowl rests in the hand. The middle fingers are placed fairly close together with the thumb much lower down the side of the bowl than in the claw grip.

Whichever grip is employed, it is important that the bowl can be held upright in the hand so that it is not leaning to the right or left.

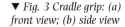

▼ *Fig. 3 Cradle grip: (a) front view; (b) side view*

(a)

(b)

Delivery

Important points

- Aim for good balance during the stance. This may be helped by keeping the feet apart.
- Do not overgrip the bowl.
- During the backswing try not to let the bowl travel away from or behind the body. Keep the bowling arm as close to the hips as possible to allow an even pendulum movement.
- The forward swing of the bowling arm, accompanied by the forward step and forward movement of the body, should be smooth and controlled.
- Make sure the knees are bent sufficiently to allow the body to be close to the playing surface, ensuring that the bowl is released smoothly without wobble or bounce.
- Complete the delivery action with a flowing follow through.
- Above all, keep the action simple. Any unnecessary movement just causes more problems.

Stance and foot faults

A player shall take his stance on the mat and at the moment of delivering his bowl shall have one foot remaining entirely within the confines of the mat. The foot may be either in contact with or over the mat. Failure to observe this Law constitutes foot-faulting. Penalty for foot-faulting: after a caution the bowl is stopped and removed to the bank.

Forehand shots

For a right-handed player the forehand shot is made when the bowl is delivered along a line which will cause it to travel in a curve from right to left.

Backhand shots

For a right-handed player the backhand shot is made when the bowl is delivered along a line which will cause it to travel in a curve from left to right.

Bias

Each bowl has an in-built bias. The bias side of the bowl is indicated by the smaller of the two discs that are stamped into the bowl. It should be remembered that this smaller disc must always appear on the inside for forehand or backhand shots. In other words, imagine a line drawn right through the centre of the rink, then always ensure that the small disc is facing that line.

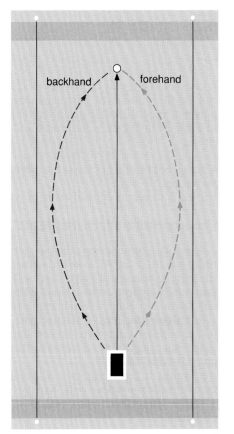

▶ *Fig. 4 The right-hander's forehand and backhand*

The game

A game of bowls may be played on one rink or the number of players taking part may be sufficient to occupy several rinks. The game continues until either:

● an agreed number of shots has been played or
● a team scores an agreed number of points or
● an agreed period of time has expired.

When the game is restricted to one rink only it is called a single game, though the number of players on each side may vary from one to four. With one player on each side the game is called **single-handed** or **singles**, with two it is **pairs**, with three **triples** and with four players on each side the game is called **fours**.

It is worth repeating that a *single* game means one game only, whereas a *singles* game means one player on each side.

There are, in addition, three other arrangements of play:

● a side game which is played over several rinks by two opposing sides, each side having the same number of players
● a series of single games or team games arranged either as knockout or league competitions and accommodating single-handed, pairs, triples or fours
● a tournament of games in which the contestant sides or teams play each other in turn.

Starting the game

The captains in a side game or skips in a team game shall toss to decide which side shall play first, but in all singles games the opponents shall toss, the winner having the option of decision.

In all ends subsequent to the first the winner of the preceding scoring end shall play first.

The player to play first delivers the jack. If the jack be delivered to a distance less than 2 m from the opposite ditch it shall be moved out so that the front of the jack (facing the players) is 2 m from the ditch, and centred.

Should the jack be delivered into the ditch or outside the boundary of the rink or less than 21 m in a straight line of play from the front of the mat, the opposing player may then remove the mat in line of play (subject to Law 26 – see page 4) and deliver the jack but shall not play first. Should the jack be improperly delivered twice, by each player in any end, it shall not be delivered again, but shall be centred so that the front of the jack is a distance of 2 m from the opposite ditch, and the mat placed at the option of the first to play.

The singles game

Each player has four bowls and plays them singly and alternately. Player X in fig. 5 having won the toss *may* deliver the jack and then deliver the first bowl. Player Y delivers his first bowl, player X follows and so on until both players have delivered their four bowls.

All bowls nearer to the jack than an opponent's nearest bowl, at the conclusion of the end, count one shot each. The maximum score for an end is four.

The end is completed when all the bowls have been played in one direction and the shots have been mutually agreed. A fresh end is then started by playing back along the rink.

The player first reaching 21 shots wins the game.

The pairs game

Each player has four bowls and plays them singly and in turn.

A and B are playing X and Y in fig. 6. A and X alternate until they have each delivered four bowls; then B and Y alternate until they have sent down four bowls each.

All bowls of one pair nearer to the jack than any bowl of the two opponents count one shot each. The maximum score for an end is eight shots. The game is concluded when the agreed number of ends has been played, the pair with the highest score being the winners.

▲ *Fig. 5 The singles game*

▼ *Fig. 6 The pairs game*

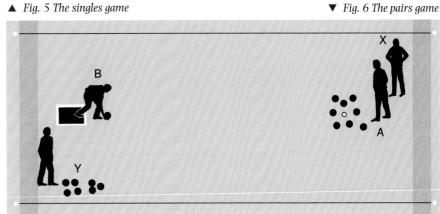

The triples game

Each player usually has three bowls and plays them singly and in turn. The first players of each team deliver their bowls alternately; the second players in each team follow; then the final players deliver their bowls.

All bowls of one team nearer to the jack than any bowl of the three opponents count one shot each. The maximum score for an end is nine shots.

The triples game usually concludes when the agreed number of ends has been played, the team with the highest score being the winners.

The fours game

Each side consists of four players, each player having two bowls and playing them singly and in turn, as in triples.

All bowls of one team nearer to the jack than any bowl of the four opponents count one shot each. The maximum score for an end is eight shots.

The game concludes in the same way as the triples game, the team with the highest score being the winners.

Movement of bowls

When a bowl has been properly delivered by a player and comes to rest, it is said to be either **live** or **dead**. If it touches the jack during its course it becomes a **toucher**. A bowl which does not touch the jack is a **non-toucher**.

Touchers

A bowl which, in its original course on the green, touches the jack is called a toucher (*see* fig. 7). It remains a 'live' bowl (*see* fig. 8) even though it passes into the ditch, provided it comes to rest in that part of the ditch within the boundaries of the rink. A toucher in the ditch may be marked by a white or a coloured peg, about 50 mm broad and not more than 100 mm in height, placed upright on the top of the bank.

If the jack should be driven into the ditch by a toucher and comes to rest there, no subsequent bowl in the end being played can become a toucher.

A toucher shall be clearly marked or indicated with a chalk mark by a member of the player's side. If a bowl is not so marked before the succeeding bowl comes to rest it ceases to be a toucher.

Care should be taken to remove toucher marks from the bowls before the playing of the succeeding end. Should a bowl be played with such marks not removed the marks shall be removed immediately the bowl comes to rest, except if such bowl has become a toucher at the end of play.

As will be seen later, if the jack has been driven into the ditch and should be displaced from its position in the ditch by a bowl delivered later in the end, i.e. by a non-toucher, it is restored to its former position in the ditch. If a later bowl drives a toucher, still lying on the green, into the ditch, displacing the jack lying in the ditch, the jack is not restored to its former position. The same rule applies if the toucher driven into the ditch displaces another toucher lying there.

Live bowl

A bowl which travels 14 m or more from the front of the mat and comes to rest within the boundaries of the rink is called a live bowl (*see* fig. 8). A live bowl is in play.

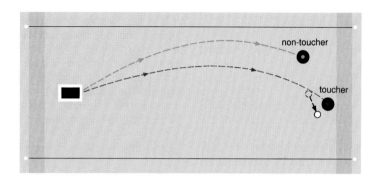

▲ *Fig. 7 A toucher and a non-toucher*   ▼ *Fig. 8 A live bowl*

Dead bowl

A dead bowl is one which:

- travels less than 14 m from the front of the mat
- finishes in the ditch not having touched the jack
- comes to rest so that the whole of the bowl is outside the boundaries of the rink or
- has been driven beyond the side boundaries of the rink by another bowl.

A toucher becomes a dead bowl if:

- it comes to rest so that the whole of the bowl is outside the boundaries of the rink or
- it has been driven beyond the side boundaries of the rink by another bowl.

A bowl must be removed from the rink and placed on the bank immediately it is accounted dead.

Should a player carry a bowl to the jack end of the rink, that bowl does not become a dead one.

It is permissible for a bowl to travel beyond the side boundary of the rink and return again to the rink without becoming dead, provided it comes to rest with part, if not the whole, of the bowl within the rink. Under no circumstances shall a boundary thread be lifted while the bowl is in motion.

Rebounding bowl

Touchers which rebound from the bank to the rink remain live bowls and continue in play.

Non-touchers rebounding from the bank to the rink become dead bowls. Similarly, non-touchers rebounding from the jack lying in the ditch, or from touchers lying in the ditch, become dead bowls.

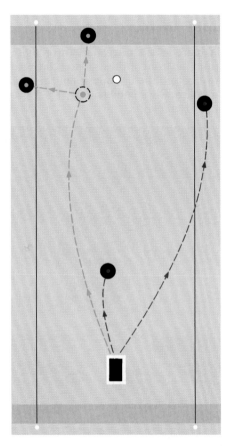

▶ *Fig. 9 Dead bowls*

Line bowls

A bowl is not considered to be outside a circle or line unless it is entirely clear of it. This is decided by looking perpendicularly down upon the bowl, or by placing a square on the green, or by use of a string, mirror or other approved optical device.

Thus, bowl A in fig. 10 is entirely beyond the side boundary and is dead; bowl C is entirely inside and is live; bowl B lies partly over the side boundary thread and, although most of the bowl is beyond the side boundary, it is live.

Again, the circle round the jack represents the inner edge of the bowl Z. Bowl X is entirely outside the circle, and is further from the jack than bowl Z; bowl Y lies partly over the circle and is therefore nearer the jack than bowl Z.

▶ *Fig. 10 Line bowls*

Displaced bowls

If a bowl is displaced from its position by a non-toucher rebounding from the bank it should be restored as near as possible to its original position by a player of the opposing side.

Players must take great care not to disturb live bowls until the end has been completed and shots awarded. Should a player taking part in the game interfere with a bowl still in motion, or displace a live bowl at rest on the green or toucher in the ditch, the captain of the opposing side can choose one of four courses of action.

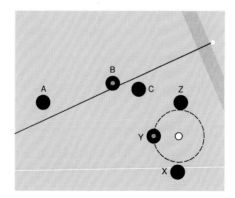

He may:

- restore the bowl as near as possible to its former position
- let it remain where it rests
- declare the bowl dead
- declare the end dead.

Should a bowl be moved when it is being marked, or measured, it must be restored to its former position by an opponent. If displacement is caused by a marker or umpire, the marker or umpire shall replace the bowl.

Bowls in motion, or live bowls at rest – including touchers in the ditch – which suffer interference or displacement by a person not playing in the rink or by a bowl played from another rink, should be placed in a position acceptable to the two captains. If the captains are unable to reach agreement the end is declared dead and is played again in the same direction. Similar action is taken if a bowl in motion, or at rest on the green, suffers interference or displacement by any object lying on the green or interfering with the game.

Movement of jack

An end is started by the delivery of the jack along the centre line of the rink. If the jack comes to rest less than 2 m from the front ditch it is repositioned as stated on page 10. While the jack remains within the boundaries of the rink, it is said to be live; if it is driven beyond the boundaries of the rink, it becomes dead.

Live jack in ditch

If a jack be driven into the ditch within the limits of the rink it shall be accounted live, and shall not be moved except by a toucher. Its place shall be marked by a white peg about 50 mm broad, and not more than 100 mm in height, and placed immediately in line with and on top of the bank, above the place where the jack rests.

Dead jack

The jack becomes dead if it is driven by the bowl in play:

- over the bank
- over the side boundary
- into an opening or inequality of any kind in the bank or
- so that it rebounds to a distance less than 18 m in a direct line from the centre of the front edge of the mat in its rebounded position.

A jack which is driven partly over a boundary thread, but not wholly beyond it, remains in play.

When the jack is dead, the end is declared dead and must be played again in the same direction, unless both skips or opponents agree to play in the opposite direction. The rule applies even if all the bowls have been played.

Boundary jack

A jack driven to the side boundary, but not wholly beyond it, remains live and in play. In such a position, the jack may be played to from either side, even though the bowl passes outside the side limits of the rink.

A bowl played at a boundary jack which comes to rest within the limits of the rink remains live and in play.

If a bowl comes to rest outside the side boundary of the rink, after it has been played at a boundary jack, it becomes dead. The result is the same even if the bowl touches the jack and then comes to rest beyond the boundary, or comes to rest touching the jack but wholly beyond the side boundary.

Damaged jack

Should the jack become damaged during play, the end is declared dead and is played again in the same direction using a new jack.

Rebounding jack

If the jack is driven against the bank and rebounds on to the rink it remains in play. Similarly, if the jack is lying in the ditch and it is operated on by a toucher so that it returns on to the rink, it remains in play.

Displaced jack

If the jack is displaced from its position by a non-toucher rebounding from the bank it should be restored, as near as possible, to its original position by a player of the opposing side.

If the jack has been played into the ditch and it is displaced from its position by a non-toucher, then the jack must be restored to its marked position by a player of the opposing side.

Should the jack be diverted from its course while it is moving on the green, i.e. after it has been struck by a bowl, the captain of the opposing side can choose one of three courses of action. He may:

• have the jack restored to its former position
• allow it to remain where it rests or
• declare the end dead.

He has a similar choice should the jack be disturbed by an opponent when it is at rest on the green or in the ditch.

A jack in motion, or at rest on the green or in the ditch, which suffers displacement by a person not playing on the rink, or by a bowl played from another rink, should be placed in a position acceptable to the two captains. If they cannot reach agreement on its position the end is declared dead. Similar action is taken if the jack is displaced by any object lying on the green or in the ditch.

Fours play

The basis of the game of bowls is fours play. This book has already mentioned the singles, pairs and triple games, all of which enjoy their popularity, particularly when there are insufficient players immediately available to form a fours. The fours game is, however, the most popular one, since it accommodates the maximum number of players – eight – on a rink, demanding that each team of four players should combine to play as a team. Matches are invariably played as fours games.

Fours play demands a greater skill than the other games. Each player is limited to two bowls, and with only a pair of bowls to deliver in each end, no player can afford to be careless with either shot.

The four players in each team are known as **lead**, **second**, **third** and **skip**. They play in that order, alternating their shots with their opposite numbers in the other teams, and continue to play in that order until the end of

17

the game or match. Changing the order involves forfeiture of the game or match to the opponents.

Each player must be a specialist in his position. In addition each player has certain duties to contribute towards the smooth progress of the game.

The lead

His special responsibility is to place the mat and deliver the jack, ensuring that the jack is centred before playing his first bowl. To commence the game the mat is placed with the front edge 2 m from the rear ditch; at subsequent ends the front edge of the mat shall be not less than 2 m from the rear ditch and not less than 23 m from the front ditch and on the centre line of the rink of play.

If his side has won the preceding end, the lead is in a position to place the mat and deliver the jack to a length preferred by his four – a big advantage.

He must be a skilful player at any length. With an open jack to play at, his object must be to get both bowls nearer the jack than any bowls delivered by his opponents. The choice of hands – backhand or forehand – rests with the lead; he should decide which hand most suits his team.

The second

The duties undertaken by the second man consist of keeping a record of all shots scored for and against his side, and retaining possession of the score card whilst play is in progress. He records the names of the players on the score card, and after each end he compares his record of the game with that of the opposing second player. At the close of the game he hands the score card to the skip.

As a player the second specialises in positioning. If the lead has placed a bowl nearer the jack the second should play his bowl into a protecting position. If the lead has lost the shot he must attempt to place his bowls closest to the jack. Versatility is required of him – an ability to play almost any shot in the game.

The third

The third player may have deputed to him the duty of measuring all disputed shots. The third man needs to be an experienced player, who must be ready for forceful play but who can, when necessary, play any shot in the game.

The skip

The skip has sole charge of his rink and his instructions must be obeyed by his players. He decides, with the opposing skip, all disputed points and their agreed decision is final. If the two skips are unable to agree, the point in dispute is referred to an umpire whose decision is final.

In the game the skip plays last. While his players are delivering their bowls he issues directions to them by hand movements. It is he who decides the tactics and strategy of his four.

Position of players during play

Possession of the rink belongs to each side in turn, belonging, at any moment, to the side whose bowl is being played. As soon as each bowl comes to rest, possession of the rink is transferred to the other side unless a bowl becomes a toucher when possession is not transferred until the toucher has been marked.

Players not in possession of the rink must not interfere with their opponents, distract their attention, or in any way annoy them.

The position of players during play is important. Players standing at the head of the green, unless directing play, i.e. the skip or third man, must stand behind the jack and away from the head. The skip or third man directing play may stand in front of the jack, but must retire behind it as soon as the bowl is delivered.

All players at the mat end of the green, other than the one actually delivering a bowl, must stand behind the mat.

Consider fig. 11. Player A, having played his bowl, is standing in front of the mat, though to one side. Although not obstructing B, he is distracting him. The rules stipulate that he should stand back, behind the mat, like C and D.

W is standing in front of the jack, though to the side. He should stand behind the jack, behind X, who is skip to B. Players Y and Z are standing in proper positions.

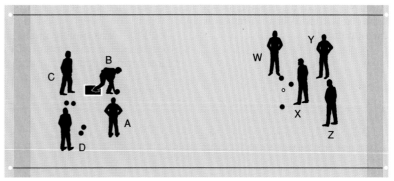

▶ *Fig. 11 Position of players in fours play*

Playing out of turn

All players must stick rigorously to their order of play in each end. If a player plays out of turn, the opposing skip may:

• stop the bowl while it is still running and have it played in its proper turn or
• if the bowl has displaced the jack or a bowl, accept the situation or, alternatively, have the end declared dead.

Playing the wrong bowl

A bowl played by mistake shall be replaced with the player's own bowl by the opponent.

Changing bowls

A player shall not be allowed to change his bowls during the course of the game, or in a resumed game, unless they be objected to, as provided in Law 9(c), or when a bowl has been so damaged in the course of play as, in the opinion of the umpire, to render the bowl (or bowls) unfit to play.

Interruptions

The umpire may stop a game, or the teams may mutually agree to cease play, on account of the weather, or because of darkness. When the game is resumed the score will be as it was when the interruption occurred, an end that was not completed not being counted. On resumption, if one of the four original players in the rink is not available, one substitute player is allowed.

Result of the end

The bowl or bowls nearer to the jack than any of the opponents' bowls are the scoring ones. In a game of winning ends the side with the bowl nearest the jack in each end becomes the winner of that end, i.e. they are awarded the shot. Otherwise all bowls nearer the jack than any of the opponents' bowls count one shot each.

To allow all the bowls to come finally to rest, up to half a minute after the last bowl has stopped running may be claimed by either side before counting the shots.

The jack or bowls may not be moved until the skips have agreed the number of shots. Exception is made, however, where a bowl must be moved to allow the measuring of another bowl.

If the nearest bowl of each team should be touching the jack, or they are agreed to be the same distance from the jack, the end is declared drawn and no score is recorded. The end is counted as a played end.

Great care must be taken when measuring a bowl to ensure that the positions of other bowls are not disturbed. If the bowl to be measured is resting on another bowl which prevents the measurement, the players must use the best available means to secure it in its position before removing the other bowl. Similar action should be taken where more than two bowls are involved or where measurement is likely to cause a single bowl to fall over or change its position.

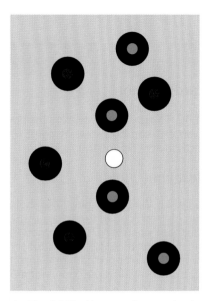

▲ *Fig. 13 The blue team has two bowls nearer the jack than the red team. The blue team scores 2 shots. If played as 'winning ends', the blue team scores 1 shot*

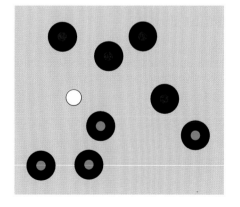

◄ *Fig. 12 The blue team has one bowl nearer the jack than the red team. The blue team scores 1 shot. If played as 'winning ends', the blue team scores 1 shot*

Game decisions

In a game of winning ends, the victory decision goes to the side or team with the majority of winning ends. For other games, the victory decision goes to the side or team with the highest total of shots.

The above decisions apply to:

- a single game
- a team or side game played on one occasion
- any stage of an eliminating competition.

In tournament games, or games in series, victory goes to the side or team with the highest number of winning ends or the highest net score of shots, according to the rules of the tournament or series of games.

If, in an eliminating competition, the score is equal when the agreed number of ends has been played, an extra end or ends are played until a decision is reached.

Shots

Draw shot

This is the most basic but also the most important shot in a bowler's repertoire. Drawing a bowl is delivering it along the correct line and with sufficient pace (or 'weight') to reach the objective. Draw shots are not bowled exclusively to the jack but can be played to an opponent's bowl or to a particular spot on the rink.

The majority of shots employed in a game of bowls will be variations on the draw shot.

Trail shot

In fig. 14 the bowler wishes to move the jack from point Y to point X. He has therefore decided to impart sufficient pace to the bowl that it will come to rest at point X, carrying the jack along with it.

Yard on shot

In fig. 15 the bowler delivers his bowl so that it comes to rest at point Y, a yard (metre) behind the jack.

Rest shot

In fig. 16 the bowler plays the shot so that his bowl comes to rest against his opponent's bowl (A). On occasion this can help to increase the number of scoring bowls or provide some form of 'insurance' against the opponent moving the jack to his own bowl (A).

Wrest shot

Here the object is to displace an opponent's bowl, ensuring that your bowl takes its place (*see* fig. 17).

Promotion shot

In fig. 18 the bowler wishes to push his own bowl (A) closer to the jack. An accurate assessment of weight is vital, especially when the way in which bowl A has come to rest is taken into consideration, i.e. if it has fallen on to its side, then fractionally more weight will be necessary than if it were on its running surface.

Plant shot

By striking his own bowl (A) in fig. 19 with sufficient pace, the bowler can dislodge the opponent's bowl (B).

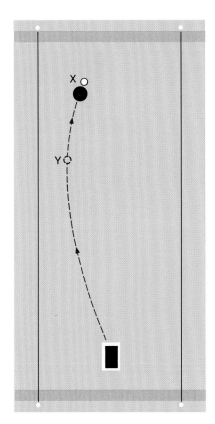

▲ *Fig. 14 Trail shot*

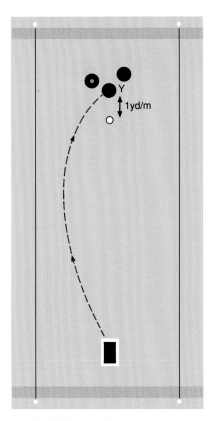

▲ *Fig. 15 Yard on shot*

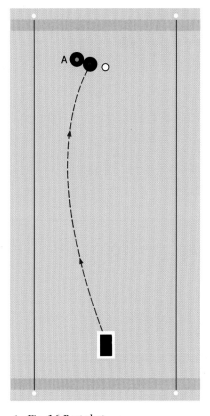

▲ *Fig. 16 Rest shot*

23

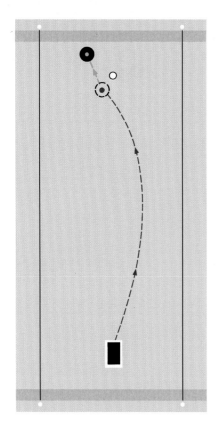

▲ Fig. 17 Wrest shot

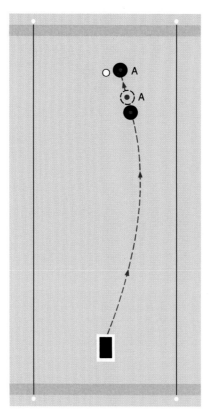

▲ Fig. 18 Promotion shot

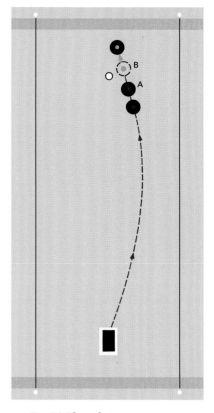

▲ Fig. 19 Plant shot

Blocking shot

This is a drawing shot which comes to rest well short of the head to prevent an opponent using driving weight to break up the head (*see* fig. 20).

Ditch weight shot

In fig. 21 the jack is in the ditch and live. The bowler delivers his bowl with sufficient pace that it comes to rest at the lip of the ditch. The bowl should not fall into the ditch since then it would be declared a dead bowl.

The trail, yard on, rest, wrest, promotion, plant, blocking and ditch weight shots are all variations on the draw shot.

The following shots result from situations in which playing with controlled weight is required to achieve an objective.

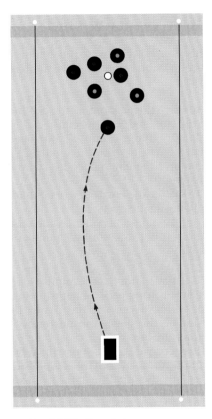

▲ *Fig. 20 Blocking shot*

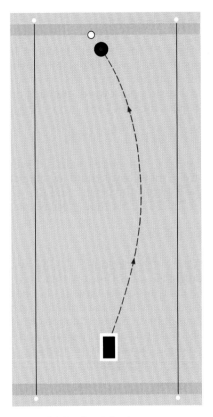

▲ *Fig. 21 Ditch weight shot*

25

Split shot

In fig. 22 the bowler dislodges his opponent's bowls (blue) by playing with sufficient force. His own bowl (red) travels on towards the jack and becomes the shot bowl.

Opening up shot

This is a shot played with sufficient pace to move bowls that have come to rest between the bowler and the jack (*see* fig. 23). This shot is occasionally necessary to create more options for the next shot.

Generally speaking, playing with controlled weight means that even if the shot misses its target(s) the bowl will still remain on the rink and in play (though there will be situations where this could prove to be very difficult to achieve). The same cannot be said for the drive or firing shot.

Drive or firing shot

This is a bowl delivered at optimum pace to achieve one of several objectives:

• to drive the jack out of the confines of the rink and 'kill' the end
• to play into a group of your opponent's bowls to drive them out of the head and thereby reduce his score at that end
• to scatter the bowls in a head that is building against you
• to take out an opponent's bowl that is preventing you scoring a number of shots.

With all shots that require controlled or firing pace an adjustment of line will be necessary. The greater the speed of the bowl, the narrower or tighter the line.

It is crucial to ask yourself, 'When should such a shot be employed?' Certainly the situation at the head and the overall score will be two important factors, but it is not good practice to always leave such a bowl until last. Do not defer the decision because a head can begin to look menacingly against you after only two of your opponent's bowls have been played. Having made a decision positively, play the shot confidently.

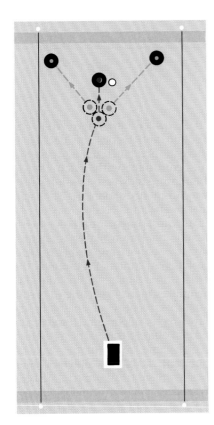

▲ *Fig. 22 Split shot*

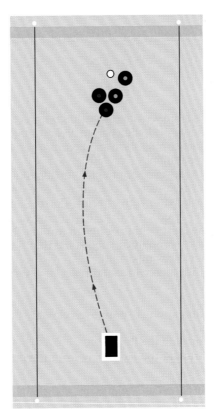

▲ *Fig. 23 Opening up shot*

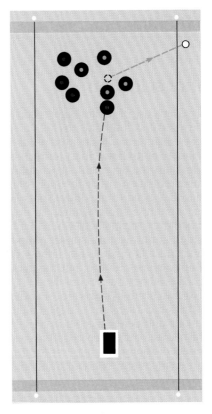

▲ *Fig. 24 Firing shot*

Tactics

Shot selection

A player's use of tactics is governed by the level of skill that he has to offer. In very basic terms, the player needs to get more of his bowls in a scoring position than his opponent. It is equally important for players to understand that they need to maximise shots *for*, and minimise shots against. To draw or achieve a second bowl when there is a high count against is a very important and telling shot: not only is the count against reduced, but the player receives a boost to his confidence.

No two heads in bowls are ever exactly the same. Therefore, to exploit all the options and percentage shots a player will need to be well prepared with a wide variety of shots at his disposal. Strategy can change from one end to another; the more versatile player has the greater chance of shifting play to his advantage. Practice must form an important part of preparation.

A player about to play the first bowl must be clear as to where he wishes his bowl to come to rest. Correct line and length need to be employed. A bowl just behind or just in front of the jack represents a good start: that first bowl is so important.

An opponent could react in several different ways, by:

- attempting to draw even closer to the jack
- moving the first bowl
- trailing the jack away from the first bowl.

It is evident, therefore, that shot selection and tactics are decided by where the first bowl comes to rest. So it can continue with each bowler attempting to wrest the advantage away from his opponent. Such play calls for effective decision making.

The most important bowl in the game is the one a player is about to play. It is almost impossible to detail the different kinds of situations that could arise. Some players may find themselves merely reacting to certain situations because of the skills displayed by an opponent. However, one end can change the course or pattern of any game, so no matter what an opponent is doing bowlers must always attempt to be disciplined and controlled, and keep drawing whenever possible in an effort to get the shot.

Pre-visualisation

Some bowlers employ a 'pre-visualisation' technique. They 'see' their bowl travelling along the green and they have a definite and clear picture of it coming to rest at a precise spot. The stronger the mental image, the better prepared is the bowler to play the shot. Often bowlers will utter a statement such as, 'I can see it this way', and this is true: they can 'see' it and will play the shot with great confidence.

This technique is particularly important when a bowl has to travel around a bowl, or indeed pass through a gap between bowls.

Reading an opponent

From the first moment bowlers begin to 'read' an opponent. They will attempt to gather as much information about him as a person, and also as a player, as possible.

- What are his strengths?
- What are his weaknesses?
- How does he respond to a slice of bad luck?
- How does he respond to a stroke of good luck?
- Is he stronger on one hand than the other?
- Does he prefer to play a particular hand or length?

All of this information helps to generate a 'player profile', to be stored and implemented when necessary. However, any implementation should never bend the rules or ignore the code of etiquette.

Common faults

Grip

It is vital that the grip is a comfortable one: it will usually fall between the claw and the cradle versions. It is advisable not to overgrip the bowl, as this will result in strain on the hand and wrist. The grip must offer comfortable control.

A fault that can occur stems from the incorrect positioning of the little finger. If this is too high on the side of the bowl, then the bowl could be wobbled on release.

Another factor that could cause the bowl to wobble is not holding it upright in the hand. If it is leaning to either right or left, then it is not rolled off the fingers on its full running surface.

Stance

A solid stance provides a well balanced and relaxed platform for the smooth delivery of the bowl. Of course, there is a variety of stances adopted by players generally, located between the upright and fixed forms. The upright stance demands the whole body be part of the delivery action, whereas with the fixed stance only the bowling arm will need to move.

Height, weight, general build, suppleness of knee, hip, wrist and shoulder joints will all have their part to play in the stance adopted by an individual. However, to provide good balance ensure that the feet are not too close together, because this will narrow the base considerably and will not provide a sound platform for any forward movement of the body.

Stance also has a say in the final result of the delivery. It is when adopting his stance on the mat that a player takes an opportunity to align his body along the path he has determined the bowl needs to travel. For a right-handed player the right foot should point along the selected line, then the left foot can be brought alongside it. A casual or indifferent placing of the right foot can lead to loss of line.

Limit any unnecessary physical movement from the moment the stance is adopted – keep the whole motion simple and straightforward. Never underestimate the importance of a well balanced stance.

Backswing

The backswing is simply a pendulum movement in a backward direction, with the bowling arm travelling close to the hip. Some players hold the bowl away from the body before beginning the backswing, but this can result in the bowling arm travelling even further away from the body during the backswing. A correction is then required when the arm moves forwards to deliver the bowl along the correct line.

There are also bowlers who hold the bowl in front of the body so that during the backswing they have to negotiate the hip, and often at the end of the backswing the bowl will be hidden by the body. This will result in the arm being moved forwards with an outward curve which, again, is not conducive to delivering along the correct line. It is better for the elbow of the bowling arm to rest close to the hip, with the bowl pointing along the right line.

An abbreviated backswing (one that does not clear the hip) can result in the bowl being *pushed* rather than rolled away. Consequently the bowl may be delivered to an unsatisfactory length. It is easier to feel a better weight control with a smooth pendulum forward movement than with a pushing action.

When playing a shot that requires increased pace or weight, many bowlers will increase the length of backswing. But this is undesirable if the speed of the backswing is such that it results in a bowl badly delivered in a jerky as opposed to a smooth action. The backswing should always be controlled, and if extra pace or weight is needed then the bowler should concentrate on bringing the bowling arm through at a faster rate.

However, at this point care must be taken to see that the faster forward action is not accompanied by a forward lunge of the body which can lead to loss of balance at the exact moment when everything should be perfectly balanced.

Some bowlers twist the wrist during the backswing. This would seem to aid the keeping of the bowling arm close to the hip. However, it must be remembered that during the forward movement of the bowling arm the wrist must be *untwisted*. This twisting of the wrist is a personal quirk; it is easier to keep to a simple pendulum motion.

Forward swing

The forward swing should be smooth and unhurried, disciplined and controlled. Any jerkiness in movement will result in a poorly delivered bowl.

The speed of the arm will be determined by the pace that the player wishes to impart to the bowl. A firing shot will dictate that the arm comes through much faster but never with loss of control. Some players are inclined to accelerate the speed of the arm over the last half-metre of the forward swing. This can result in the bowl being lobbed out of the hand rather than rolled off the fingers.

For those who do not adopt a fixed stance, the forward swing is accompanied by body movement in a forward direction. This movement must be controlled or loss of balance could ensue. Bending the knees also helps to lower the body closer to the green to ensure a smooth release of the bowl,

During the swing the shoulder, elbow, wrist and hand of the bowling arm must face the chosen line. The arm should therefore be kept close to the body.

Forward step

Some bowlers will take the forward step simultaneously with the backswing; others will take it as they are completing the forward swing. It is a matter of personal choice. Others may split the forward stride into two movements by placing the leading foot ahead of the back foot even before they begin the backswing. Therefore, on completion of the forward swing only a minimal forward movement need be taken by the leading foot.

The length of the forward stride need not be more than a walking pace. There are those who step a little further and others who exceed it by quite a margin. A long forward stride results in considerable body weight being added to the delivery action; if this is not strictly controlled, it could result in a poor shot. The body must be perfectly balanced on release of the bowl and an excessively long forward stride is not always conducive to the maintenance of good balance.

It has already been suggested that bending the knees even before the backswing can lower the body nearer to the playing surface. This lowering of the body will provide extra control on the forward step, since it is more difficult to take a long forward stride when the body is closer to the green.

The placing of the forward foot is vital, too. If it is placed directly in line with the back foot, it provides a very narrow base for balance. Ensure the leading foot is placed parallel to a line extending from the back foot. This could also assist the bowler in finding the right line for the bowl on delivery.

One of the most common faults in the placing of the forward foot is to have it angled across the body. On the forehand (for a right-handed player) this may result in the bowling arm being hooked at the point of release, leading to an incorrect line. On the backhand (for a right-handed player) a similar placing of the forward foot may result in an outward twisting of the bowling hand to avoid contact with the leading foot; again, correct line will be lost.

Due to problems with knee or hip joints, some players elect to play off the 'wrong' foot, i.e. a right-handed player steps forwards with the right foot. This does not contravene any law; it is a matter of personal choice.

Release

The correct timing of the release of the bowl is critical: a fraction too soon or too late can result in the bowl being bumped on delivery. Such a bump could distort the pace of the bowl, since it is not rolled smoothly off the platform provided by the hand.

On release some players tend to flick the wrist, which results in the bowl being lobbed out of the hand. Others flick the fingers, probably in an effort to impart more pace to the bowl. Neither method aids a smooth delivery.

The exact point of release will vary from player to player, but it should not be behind the leading foot or indeed too far ahead of it. As a form of practice, go through the delivery action without a bowl – the point where the fingers brush the floor is likely to be the one which suits the individual player.

Follow through

Players who use a follow through display many differences in style.

The follow through should be the natural completion of the forward swing. Place a coin on the palm of the bowling hand and swing the arm forwards to lob the coin out of the hand. The result is that the palm remains uppermost, with the arm pointing along the line taken by the coin.

Some bowlers complete the follow through by bringing the arm across the body. If this movement is begun a fraction of a second too early, it can result in a hooking action, so remember to deliver the bowl correctly before the swing across the body commences.

Those who take too long a forward stride may find they cannot follow through because loss of balance will necessitate the bowling hand being placed on the playing surface in order to prevent toppling over.

There are as many individual follow through actions as there are delivery styles. Players must find the one that best suits their delivery action.

Position of the head

As in most ball games, the correct positioning of the head in bowls is vital.

If, at the moment of release, the player drops his head and looks downwards, the result may be loss of line.

If the head bobs up swiftly at the split second of release, the bowl may be bumped along the green. In this instance a player should discipline himself to watch the bowl for at least 7–9 m before bringing up his head.

Although the head needs to be still, it should not be held in a rigid fashion. The position needs to be comfortable and relaxed. All players have an optimum distance they can look along the green with the maximum degree of comfort. Find that point. Look beyond it and you will be holding your head too high. This will generate tension in the neck and shoulders, which will be transmitted to the bowling arm.

Any unnecessary movement of the head will affect the shoulders, arms and overall balance. Therefore, it is always important to keep the head as still and yet as comfortable as possible.

Non-bowling arm

The whole of the body is involved in the delivery action, so the non-bowling arm must not be ignored.

It must not be allowed to wave about during the delivery action, because this could have a detrimental effect on overall balance. If the arm is allowed to be free during delivery, then it needs to be placed in almost the same spot each time. However, several bowlers have overcome this problem by choosing to place the non-bowling hand on the thigh of the leading leg. Some may place it on the knee of that leg, while others will use this same action as support for the upper body. These measures offer forms of control over the non-bowling arm which are far more acceptable than allowing it to be wayward and thus possibly contributing to poor delivery.

Rear leg and foot

The rear leg and foot form a crucial factor in good balance. Many players prefer to keep the foot anchored on the mat, while others will raise it at the moment of release. This is a question of individual style. Raising the foot is acceptable, providing it does not contravene the law on foot-faulting.

A point to consider is the initial stance on the mat. Some players will stand at the back end of the mat, thereby having to take a long forward step to reach the playing surface. There is nothing essentially wrong in this unless it results in loss of balance.

Young bowlers who are sufficiently supple will keep the rear foot on the mat but allow the knee to tuck in behind the front leg. This can provide a narrow base for balance but their suppleness allows them to do this without any apparent strain or discomfort.

Others will end their delivery action by balancing on the toes of the rear foot which may cause the body to wobble slightly, once more resulting in imbalance.

Duties of marker

In a fours or triples game the second player keeps the score; in a pairs game either of the partners may function as scorer; in a singles game the score should be kept by a marker. During the playing of each end he remains at the jack end of the rink and, in addition to keeping the score, he performs the following duties.

- The marker shall control the game in accordance with the WBB/IBB Basic Laws. He shall, before play commences, examine all bowls for the imprint of the WBB/IBB stamp and/or that of its national association, such imprint to be clearly visible, and shall ascertain by measurement the width of the rink of play.
- He shall centre the jack, and shall place a full length jack 2 m from the ditch.
- He shall ensure that the jack is not less than 21 m from the front edge of the mat, after it has been centred.

- He shall stand at one side of the rink, and to the rear of the jack.
- He shall answer affirmatively or negatively a player's inquiry as to whether a bowl is jack high. If requested, he shall indicate the distance of any bowl from the jack, or from any other bowl, and also, if requested, indicate which bowl he thinks is shot and/or the relative position of any other bowl.
- He shall chalk all touchers immediately they come to rest, and mark the position of the jack and touchers in the ditch. (*See* Law 34.) With the agreement of both opponents he shall remove all dead bowls from the green and ditch.
- He shall not move, or cause to be moved, either jack or bowls until each player has agreed to the number of shots.

- He shall measure carefully all doubtful shots when requested by either player. If unable to come to a decision satisfactory to the players, he shall call in an umpire. If an official umpire has not been appointed, the marker shall select one. The decision of the umpire shall be final.
- He shall enter the score at each end, and shall intimate to the players the state of the game.
- When the game is finished, he shall see that the score card, containing the names of the players, is signed by the players, and disposed of in accordance with the rules of the competition.

Duties of umpire

An umpire shall be appointed by the controlling body of the association, club or tournament management committee. His duties shall be as follows.

- He shall, in fours, triples and pairs games, examine all bowls for the imprint of the WBB/IBB stamp, and/or that of its national association, and ascertain by measurement the width of the rinks of play.
- He shall measure any shot or shots in dispute, and for this purpose shall use a suitable measure. His decision shall be final.
- He shall decide all questions as to the distance of the mat from the ditch, and the jack from the mat.
- He shall decide as to whether or not jack and/or bowls are in play.
- He shall enforce the game's laws.

Absentee players

In a competitive single fours game where a club is represented by only one four, all the members of the four must be genuine members of the club. Unless all four players appear and are ready to play at the end of the maximum waiting period of 30 minutes, or should they introduce an ineligible player, then the team shall forfeit the match to the opposing team.

In a side game where not more than one player is absent from either side after a period of 30 minutes, the game proceeds. In the defaulting team or four, the number of bowls is made up by the lead and second players each playing three bowls. One fourth of the score made by the defaulting team or four is deducted at the end of the game.

If two or more players are absent from a four or team, play takes place only on the full fours. In a single four game the defaulting team forfeits the game.

Play interruptions

Should play be interrupted due to darkness, weather, etc., it is resumed with the scores as they were when play was stopped, an uncompleted end being declared null. If one of the original players in any four is not available when play is resumed, one substitute is permitted, but they must not be transferred from another four.

A substitute may take the place of a player who has to leave the green owing to illness. The substitute must be a member of the club to which the four belongs, and he must join the four as lead, second or third man – never as skip. Should a player in a single game become ill, the game is resumed, if possible, at a later time or date. A player may not delay play by leaving the rink except with the consent of his opponent, and then not for more than ten minutes.

Contravention of any of the above conditions entitles the opposing side to claim the game or match.

Outside influences

Spectators

Spectators must remain beyond the limits of the rink and clear of the verges, preserving an attitude of neutrality. They are not allowed to disturb or advise the players.

Objects on the green

Except for the markings of a live jack in the ditch, no extraneous object intended to assist a player may be placed on the green or rink, or on a bowl or jack.

Unforeseen incidents

If the position of the jack or bowls be disturbed by wind or a storm, and the two skips are unable to agree the replacement positions, the end is played again in the same direction.

Betting and gambling

Betting or gambling in connection with any game or games is not permitted within the grounds of any constituent club of a national association.

CROWN GREEN BOWLS

The green, bowls, jack and footer

The green may be square or oblong, varying in size with a minimum width of 25 m (metric measurements only are used for green dimensions). The surface of the green slopes upwards rising to a central crown up to 35 cm higher than the edges. The surface tends to be irregular, unlike the level surface of the rink green. The crown and surface irregularities provide fresh factors to influence the running of the bowls. The entrance to the green, which must be near the centre of one of the sides, should be clearly marked.

Each player in the game uses two bowls. The quality, size, weight and bias of the bowls are as important to the player in the crown green game as in the level green game. There are no restrictions on size, weight and bias; the player has, therefore, a greater choice of bowls. The height of the crown and the undulations on the surfaces of different greens exhibit large variations. In general, a higher crowned green requires a more heavily biased bowl than a smaller crowned green. Many players find it an advantage to have two or three sets of bowls, differently biased, and they use those most suitable to the green upon which the game is being played.

The jack corresponds in shape and bias with the bowls but it is much smaller. Standard jacks shall weigh a minimum of 20 oz (567 g) and a maximum of 24 oz (680 g), and the diameter shall be 3¾ in (95 mm) minimum, 3⅞ in (98.5 mm) maximum. In respect of all standard jacks manufactured after 1st January 1994, the minimum and maximum weight shall be 23 oz (653 g) and 24 oz (680 g) respectively, and the diameter shall be 3¹³⁄₁₆ in (97 mm) minimum, 3⅞ in (98.5 mm) maximum, and conform to the agreed standard profile.

The delivery of the jack is an important part of the game – as it runs over the green it responds to the surface and to its own bias. The player can gain much information about the irregularities and the shape of the green by watching the jack.

The footer is a round mat with a diameter not less than 5 in (128 mm) and not more than 6 in (154 mm) on which each player must place his toe when delivering the jack or bowl.

Effects of bias and crown

Both the bias and the slope of the green cause the bowls to run in curved paths. The bias on a particular bowl remains unchanged; the slope of the green varies with each shot, since two shots are rarely played over the same path.

The green will always tend to pull the bowl in the direction of the downward slope (*see* fig. 25). As the bias can be transferred from one side of the bowl to the other at the discretion of the player, the two effects of bias and green can be used together, widely curving the path of the bowl; or against one another when the path of the bowl will be less curved and may run almost straight. Almost straight, but never quite straight, for in the last foot (30 cm) or so before the bowl stops, the pull of the bias at low speed will usually be much greater than the pull of the green, and the bowl will curve round in response to the bias.

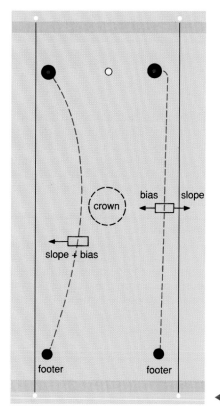

Straight peg and round peg

In a **straight peg** shot, the slope of the green and the bias of the wood are used in opposition to one another, and the bowl follows a path which can be almost straight.

In a **round peg** shot, the slope of the green and the bias are used together to increase the curvature of the path of the bowl.

◀ *Fig. 25 Effects of bias and slope*

39

Delivery

Hand restrictions

A player bowling the jack with his right hand must deliver his bowls with the right hand and have his right toes on the footer. He must continue to bowl with his right hand throughout the game.

Similarly, a player bowling the jack with his left hand must deliver his bowls and continue throughout the game with his left hand, his left toes being on the footer.

The only exception allowed to this rule is for the player who suffers a disability and for whom it would be physically impossible to observe it.

Players are not allowed to bowl with the right or left hand at will – the extra few inches of ground so gained would be a big advantage to the player in the crown green game who can play equally well with the right or left hand.

There is a penalty attached to the non-observance of this law. On the first occasion the referee should order the bowl to be stopped and played again properly. On a second or subsequent occasion the referee should declare the bowl to be dead.

Foot restrictions

The player must place and keep his toe on the footer while delivering a bowl or the jack, the toe remaining in contact with the footer until the wood has left his hand.

The game

The game is played by two players, each player having two bowls. The object of the game is to get one or both bowls nearer to the jack than either of the opponent's bowls. The bowls are delivered alternately until each player has delivered both bowls.

The jack, then, is delivered first, and thereafter the players deliver their bowls to the jack. The right to deliver the jack belongs to the player who won the preceding end; the right to deliver the first jack is decided by the spin of a coin.

The player throwing the jack in each end is called the **leader**. On starting the game the leader places the footer within 3 m of the entrance to the green and 1 m from the edge of the green. Play commences from that point, and continues over the green in all directions.

At the conclusion of the end, the footer should be placed at the jack by the last player. The leader in the succeeding end may, however, remove the footer to any position within a circle of radius 1 m, taking the jack as the centre of the circle. If he moves the footer he must do so before throwing the jack for the next end.

The footer must remain in position throughout the game. If it is taken up after playing a bowl, and that bowl has to be replayed, then the footer must be replaced as near to its former position as possible. Throughout the game each player must continue to use the jack and the bowls with which he started, except by permission of the referee, and then only if in his opinion the jack or bowls are so damaged as to be unplayable.

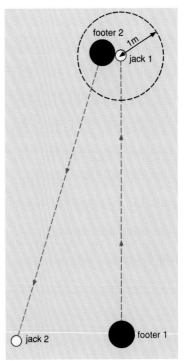

▶ *Fig. 26 Positioning the footer*

The score

The number of points to be scored to make the game is mutually agreed by the players before play starts.

The winner of each end scores one point for each of his bowls which, when both players have delivered their bowls and the bowls have come to rest, lies nearer to the jack than his opponent's nearest bowl. In fig. 27, the red player scores two points because both his bowls are nearer the jack than either of the bowls of the blue player.

When the result is in doubt and it is necessary to measure distances between the jack and the bowls, the adjustable end of the measuring pegs must be taken to the jack.

The winner of the end, and only he, signals the result to the scorers.

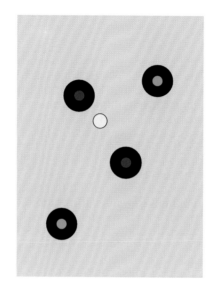

▲ *Fig. 27 Scoring an end*

The referee

Setting a mark

The functions of the referee are:

- to settle any dispute not provided for in the laws of the game
- to insist on adherence to the laws of the game
- to give decisions when the players cannot agree
- under certain circumstances, to remove a bowl so that measuring can be carried out.

If a dispute does arise which is not covered by the laws, the decision of the referee on any point is final.

The leader of each end delivers the jack and when it comes to rest the leader is said to have **set a mark**.

If the leader fails to set a mark, his opponent then attempts to do so, using the same jack. The opponent is not allowed to play first at the jack.

If the opponent fails to set a mark then the original leader has a further trial. The alternate trials continue until a mark has been set, but whoever finally sets it, the original leader plays the first bowl to it.

Not a mark

It shall not be accepted as a mark:

- if, after an objection, the jack is proved by measurement to be less than 19 m from the footer, the measurement to be taken from the nearest point of the jack to the centre of the footer
- if, when bowled, the jack goes off the green.

Objection to mark

If a player wishes to make objection to a mark he must raise his hand as a signal to the referee. There is no set form of words for questioning the legitimacy of a mark – any remark which suggests that a mark has not been set is regarded as an objection.

Objection to a mark must be made verbally **after** the first bowl has come to rest. If the measurement proves that a mark has been set play continues.

On the other hand, if the leader questions a mark set by his opponent, neither player is allowed to deliver a bowl until the objection has been settled. If the measurement proves it is a mark the leader must play to it.

Any objection to a mark must be settled by measurement – a tape or other certified measure, at least 19 m long, must be used.

Delivering the jack

The winner of an end, in addition to increasing his score, gains an advantage in the succeeding end in that he delivers the jack. By doing so, he gets a preliminary 'feel' of the green and, of course, can choose which bias, left or right, he gives to the jack. In fairness to his opponent he must not bowl the jack without allowing his opponent to see which bias he gives to the jack or to watch the course of the jack from a point near the footer.

Having observed these rules he is not compelled to tell his opponent which bias he has given the jack.

Jack off green

If the jack is struck off the green it is assumed that end has been played. Play is resumed 1 m from the point where the jack went off the green and the player who set the mark, whether he was the leader or not, delivers the jack to set a new mark.

Jack impeded or displaced

There are often several games taking place simultaneously on the green. As each game proceeds criss-cross over the green it is inevitable that some interference takes place. Provision is made for such happenings in the rules, and, in general, no penalty is incurred.

The jack must be returned and delivered again if:

- while it is still running it is impeded in any way or
- it stops on the land of the other players, i.e. is in the direct path of the bowls of another game.

If two jacks from different games are bowled near the same place, the last one to come to rest must be pronounced not a mark and returned to the players.

When a mark has been set the end becomes void if:

- the jack is displaced by a bowl or the jack of another player or
- the jack is displaced by an exterior cause, and the players are unable to agree to which spot it should be replaced.

Again, the end becomes void if a player strikes the jack with his bowl and the jack comes in contact with:

- a bowl or jack belonging to players other than his opponent or
- any person on the green.

Note that if a player strikes the jack with his bowl and the jack comes in contact with his other bowl, or with either of the opponent's bowls, it must remain at the place to which it was disturbed and the end continued.

Delivering the bowl

A player must bowl with the same hand throughout the game. If he first delivered the jack with his right hand, he must deliver his bowls with his right hand, with his right toes on the footer. Similarly, if he first delivered the jack with his left hand, he must continue to bowl with his left hand, his left toes on the footer.

Each player can retain possession of the footer until his bowl has ceased running. If the leader, for instance, sets a mark with the first delivery of the jack he maintains possession of the footer until his first bowl has ceased running; but he must not deliver his bowl until the jack has come to rest.

Many players complete their delivery by following up the bowl. If the opponent should then take possession of the footer, he must wait until the bowl has stopped running before delivering his own bowl.

Dead bowl

A bowl becomes dead if:

- it travels less than 3 m from the footer
- it is played or struck off the green
- it falls out of the player's hand, even by accident, and runs so far that it cannot be recovered without quitting the footer
- it is placed, not played
- if a bowl other than the player's own is delivered.

A bowl that becomes dead must be taken out of play immediately.

Running bowl impeded

If a running bowl is impeded, other than by the player himself, it must be played again. Should this be the leader's first bowl he may, at his discretion, have the jack returned to him to set another mark.

If a running bowl is impeded by either player, both the offending player's bowls shall be forfeited at that end.

This rule does not prohibit a player's bowl striking the jack or any bowls which have been delivered in that end.

If a mark has been set, but the leader cannot deliver his first bowl because a tape is on the green while a mark in another game is measured, he may have the jack returned and set another mark.

When it is seen that a running jack or bowl is likely to strike a still bowl or jack in another game, the running jack or bowl should be stopped, returned and replayed.

Approaching running bowl

After delivering a bowl the player must not approach nearer than 1 m to it before it stops running. If he follows it across the green he must give his opponent an uninterrupted view of the bowl in its course.

At no time must he attempt to speed it up or slow it down during its progress.

A severe penalty is attached to this rule. If a player offends, the bowl is taken out of play. On the second occasion his bowls are removed from the green and the game is awarded to his opponent, the defaulter to receive no score.

If a player is standing at the end where the jack lies he must not stand directly behind the jack nor must he obstruct the view of his opponent.

Playing wrong bowl

A bowl played out of turn must be returned and played again in its proper turn. If a bowl other than the player's own is delivered, by mistake or deliberately, it becomes a dead bowl to that player and he loses one of his bowls as a penalty. The bowl that was played is returned to the opponent to be played again by its proper owner. Should a wrongly played bowl disturb the jack or a bowl that has been played, then the disturbed bowl should be replaced as nearly as possible to its original position.

Disturbing a still bowl

Should either player touch or displace a still bowl before the end is completed, both the offending player's bowls are forfeited at that end, but if a still bowl is disturbed by any other person it must be replaced as near as possible to its original position. Similar action is taken if a still bowl is disturbed by a jack or bowl from another game.

Counting the score

Both players must be careful when counting the score at the conclusion of the end. Neither jack nor bowls can be moved until the leader and his opponents are agreed on the result, otherwise the opponent can claim a point for each of his bowls in play.

If it should be necessary, as often happens, to measure the distance between the jack and two or more bowls, care must be taken not to disturb the jack and bowls. Should a player disturb a jack or a bowl while measuring is taking place he loses the point he is claiming.

Sometimes a bowl rests on another one, or on the jack, and the measurement cannot be completed without removing the obstructing bowl. Such removals should always be made by the referee, and if the remaining bowl should move its position when the supporting bowl is removed, the player must accept its new position.

Conduct

Unfair play or ungentlemanly conduct should be punished severely by the referee. His decision on such matters is final; on the first occasion he may caution the player concerned or order him to retire from the green; on the second occasion he will certainly send him off the green. It follows that the player so punished will forfeit the game, his opponent receiving the maximum score and the offending player to receive no score. Players should note that wilful breaches of the laws of the game should be similarly punished.

Good behaviour is expected of spectators. They are not allowed on the green, and if they should encroach on the green, the players or the referee should order them off. The only persons allowed on the green are the players, the referee and the measurers when their services are required.

Interruptions

Once a game has commenced it should be played to its finish. A player may temporarily leave the green having informed his opponent and obtained the permission of the referee; should he fail to obtain that permission he forfeits the game.

If bad light or the weather causes an interruption or postponement of the game, the points scored by each player will continue to count. The position of the jack on the green should be marked so that the game may be resumed from its interrupted point. Appeals against the light or the weather should be made to the referee.

Associations

For further information on the game of bowls, contact:

English Bowling Association
Lyndhurst Road
Worthing
West Sussex
BN11 2AZ

British Crown Green
Bowling Association
94 Fishers Lane
Pensby
Wirral
L61 8SB

Index